MW01040693

Let's Make Waves!

Complete Instructions for Making Ocean Waves Quilts

Marianne Fons   **Liz Porter**

C & T Publishing

Photography by:
Perry Struse
Rural American Graphics
West Des Moines, Iowa
Sharon Risedorph
San Francisco, California
(Plates 3 and 8)
Lloyd Fons
Houston, Texas
(authors' photo)

Copyright © 1989 by Marianne Fons and Liz Porter

Illustrations and Design by Helen Young Frost
Tucson, Arizona

Typesetting: Typecraft
Tucson, Arizona

Published by C & T Publishing
P.O. Box 1456
Lafayette, California 94549

ISBN: 0-914-881-21-3

All rights reserved. No part of this work covered by the
copyright hereon may be reproduced or used in any form
or by any means — graphic, electronic, or mechanical, in-
cluding photocopying, recording, taping, or information
storage and retrieval systems without written permission
from the publisher.

Library of Congress Catalog Card No: 88-72135

Printed in the United States of America

Acknowledgements

The authors wish to acknowledge the valuable help of Barbara Brackman, Lawrence, Kansas, who shared what she knew about the history of the Ocean Waves pattern.

We would also like to thank the following persons who made Ocean Waves quilts:

Donna Brayman, Sally Cameron, Dorothy Crowdes, Luella Fairholm, Karan Flanscha, Cathy Grafton, Mary Lou Jones, Ilene Kagarice, Mary B. Larson, Jackie Leckband, Sylvia Lewis, Helen Martens, Betty Means, Martha Meyer, Mary Miller, Marilyn Parks, Jessica Peterson, Mary Remington, Joan Stuesser, Martha Street, Evalee Waltz, and the Heritage Quilters. Special thanks to Holly Girard for lending us a Bernina sewing machine in Lancaster, Pennsylvania.

For lending historic Ocean Waves quilts, we wish to thank:

Kris Cable, Julie Silber at Esprit, John and Deanna Freeberg, Madison County Historical Museum, Merry Silber and Merikay Waldvogel.

To our quilting friends,
without whom this book
(especially the quilts pictured in it)
would not have been possible.

Contents ⌇⌇⌇⌇⌇⌇⌇⌇⌇⌇⌇⌇⌇⌇⌇⌇⌇⌇⌇⌇⌇⌇⌇⌇⌇⌇⌇

Introduction

The quilt in Photo 8 of this book is the first Ocean Waves we made. It was a sweepstakes prize for *Creative Ideas for Living Magazine* in 1986. Before we started the quilt, we knew that piecing all the triangles for it would be a big job, but we planned to ease the task by working together and by using a quick machine piecing technique to sew them.

Liz brought two big bags of her rust, natural and blue fabrics to Marianne's house. We used a very unscientific method for combining fabrics for the small triangle-square units: we picked up one of Liz's prints and paired it with one of Marianne's. If we could stand to look at the two fabrics together, they were okay! Liz did the marking, Marianne the sewing. In one day, using sixty different fabrics, we pieced the almost 1,000 triangles needed for the quilt.

Working this way was so much fun we decided to make a second Waves quilt just like the first. Next thing we knew, we were putting together a third top, this time in pinks and blues. As one thing lead to another, we were soon teaching Ocean Waves workshops for quilt guilds and quilt shops in our travels around the country. We organized the class so students worked in teams of two, one person marking and cutting and one sewing. In a one-day workshop, the class would produce a full-size quilt top, which one lucky student won to take home. Other class members, we often learned, got together again to piece quilt tops for each other. Quilt guilds found they could turn out a handsome raffle quilt (well, the top anyway) in record time by joining forces for a marathon stitching session. Eventually, we also developed an all-day class that allowed each student to work on her own Ocean Waves wall quilt.

So, *Let's Make Waves!* is the culmination of lots of teamwork. It's our first joint effort since Liz's stint as an editor at Better Homes and Gardens and Marianne's solo publication, *Fine Feathers. Let's Make Waves!* is full of quilts made by us or by teams of our quilting friends.

You may use this book quite successfully to make Ocean Waves quilts on your own, or you may gather with other quilters and have a sort of "piecing bee" to create a top quickly. In any case, we hope you find using our book lots of fun and that everyone buys her own copy!

Best regards,
Liz and Marianne

Ocean Waves History

Romanticizing the Ocean Waves pattern is easy to do, even for Iowa quilters living in the middle of cornfields, with at least 1,000 miles between us and the beach in any direction. We can imagine long-ago New England quilters actually piecing their thousands of triangles as they paced the widow's walks on their seacoast houses, scanning the horizon for returning ships.

As with much quilt history, facts are few, and fancy is plentiful. We can't know for sure how Ocean Waves got its name, but the visual resemblance of a typical blue-and-muslin version, such as in Photo 1, to water and whitecaps is obvious.

Although an early pattern of nothing but right-angle triangles was called Ocean Waves in an 1889 Ladies' Art Company catalog, the familiar version constructed of small triangles along with larger setting squares and triangles is the one we think of as Ocean Waves today. Ruby McKim called it "Ocean Wave" in her 1931 book, *101 Patchwork Patterns*, and implied that the design stretched back for generations. However, dated Ocean Waves quilts (which are rare due to the pattern's typically scrap bag treatment) suggest a popularity around 1890–1916.

According to historian Barbara Brackman, Ocean Waves was popular in an era when calico was cheap and quiltmakers enjoyed combining hundreds and sometimes thousands of tiny pieces of different prints into their quilts. Her own examination of non-dated Ocean Waves quilts supports an end-of-the-nineteenth century origin.

Most historic Ocean Waves examples are cotton calico quilts, made of a variety of scraps, although many in a controlled blue and white or red and white color scheme turn up in antique shops and at quilt exhibits, too. Quiltmakers often used the Ocean Waves pattern to show off their collections of calico prints. The design was also popular with Amish quilters who avoided using prints, but often incorporated a colorful variety of cottons or wools in their Ocean Waves designs.

All seven Ocean Waves variations we've included in this book were inspired by old quilts. The Random-Scrap style pays no attention whatsoever to darks and lights, which sometimes prompts quilters to ask, "Is it still Ocean Waves?" (The answer is yes.) The type we have called Scrap-With-Constant, is a common antique variation, though sometimes the "constant" fabric is actually many very similar lights or darks. For this variation, and most of the others in the book, the proper placement of lights and darks is essential to the pattern. Pinwheel versions seem to have been popular in the 1930s. The Depression-era example in Photo 5 is a unique combination of the two Ocean Waves variations we call Pinwheel and the Wedge.

As far as we can see, no one has suggested constructing the Ocean Waves quilt the way we do. The old-fashioned system (which we assume originated when hand-piecing was the general order of the day) was to make six-sided wedges and then join these wedges to the setting pieces (Figure 1). Jinny Beyer, in *Patchwork Patterns*, offered a way (Figure 2) to avoid the setting-in that the earlier method dictated. Our method involves basically ignoring the usual concept of the Ocean Waves design and dividing the quilt into rectangular units (Figure 3). Even the variation we call the Wedge can be constructed our way with no set-in pieces.

Although you can often find straight-set Ocean Waves quilts from the past, in which setting squares are parallel to the sides of the quilt, all the versions in this book have diagonally-placed setting pieces. We feel this diagonal setting is what gives the Ocean Waves pattern its wonderful liveliness, regardless of the dark/light fabric placement used.

In our own work with the Ocean Waves design (so seemingly simple, but also easily confusing with its many hundreds of pieces and turning of triangles to make the pattern right), we cannot understand how the women of the nineteenth and early twentieth centuries were able to make this quilt without benefit of graph paper or calculator. The fact that they did amazes us and is part of what motivates us to continue learning about and experimenting with American quilts in general.

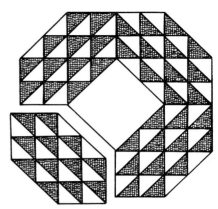

Figure 1

Figure 2

Figure 3

References:

Beyer, Jinny. *Patchwork Patterns*. McClean, VA: EPM Publications, Inc., 1979.

Bishop, *New Discoveries in American Quilts*. New York: E. P. Dutton & Company, Inc., 1975.

Brackman, Barbara, *An Encyclopedia of Pieced Quilt Patterns*. Lawrence, Kansas, 1981.

McKim, Ruby, 101 *Patchwork Patterns*. New York: Dover Publications, 1962.

Pellman, Rachel, and Kenneth Pellman. *The World of Amish Quilts*. Intercourse, Pennsylvania: Good Books, 1984.

Townsend, Louise. "The Great American Quilt Classics, Ocean Wave." *Quilters's Newsletter Magazine*, May, 1980. Wheatridge, Colorado.

1   This traditional indigo and white late nineteenth century Ocean Waves substantiates the notion that the combination of dark and light triangles is meant to represent waves and whitecaps. There are more than 2,000 single triangles in this hand-pieced classic. (Ocean Waves, 73″ x 80″, collection of John and Deanna Freeberg.)

Read This Before You Begin!

Ocean Waves is one of the many traditional American patchwork quilt patterns that has several variations. We searched through our picture books of antique quilts, and at quilt shows, with the goal of compiling a collection of Ocean Waves variations quilters would enjoy making. By following the instructions in this book, you can create "scrappy" Ocean Waves quilts that have up to sixty different fabrics, or quilts that have just two or three carefully selected prints or solids. You can make a full/queen size bed quilt, a twin bed coverlet, a wall quilt, or either of two miniature-sized quilts for doll or wall.

All the new quilts shown in the book were constructed with quick-pieced right-angle triangles, in finished sizes of either 2½" (for the bed quilts and the larger wall quilts) or 1" (for the mini-size quilts).

As we turned up different kinds of Ocean Waves quilts in our research, we gave each one a name to help us keep the variations straight. In the following pages, you'll see Ocean Waves quilts known as Random-Scrap, Scrap-With-Constant, Wedge, Two-Fabric, Contrast-Set, Pinwheel and Split-Set. The various styles have either pieced or plain fabric borders, with a particular border style assigned to each quilt. If you wish, you may substitute one border style for another, because the inner quilt sizes are the same for each variation. But remember that substituting a different border may affect the fabric requirements we have given. Also note that the cutting measurements we give for fabric borders are adequate for either mitered or straight corners.

For quick reference, the variations and the quilt sizes in this book are identified below.

Note: The outer quilt dimensions may be a few inches larger or smaller depending on which variation you choose due to the different border treatment assigned to each variation in this book. The inner quilt measurements are the same regardless of variation.

Random-Scrap

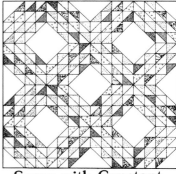

Scrap-with-Constant

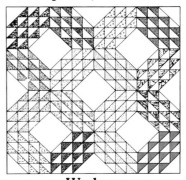

Wedge

Sizes:

Full/Queen Quilt
80" x 100"
Inner quilt is always 60" x 80"

Twin Coverlet
60" x 80"
Inner quilt is always 40" x 60"

Wall Quilt
50" x 50"
Inner quilt is always 40" x 40"

Doll Quilt
24" x 32"
Inner quilt is always 16" x 24"

Mini Wall Quilt
24" x 24"
Inner quilt is always 16" x 16"

Variations:

Two-Fabric

Contrast-Set

Pinwheel

Split-Set

General Instructions

Quick-pieced Triangle-squares for Ocean Waves Quilts

With the grid method of quick-piecing right-angle triangles into squares (we call them triangle-squares), two fabrics are placed right sides together, triangles are marked, and diagonal seams sewn before cutting. Using a grid method is not only faster and easier, but is also generally more accurate than marking, cutting, and stitching individual triangles. Sewing before cutting also helps prevent stretching the bias fabric edges of the triangles, a common problem when sewing individual pairs of triangles. The many triangle-squares of the Ocean Waves variations in this book can all be quick-pieced using grids.

The quilts in this book can be divided into two categories, those that use lots of fabrics (Random-Scrap, Scrap-With-Constant and Wedge), and those that use only two or three fabrics (Two-Fabric, Contrast-Set, Pinwheel and Split-Set). The same grid arrangements can be used for all the scrap-type quilts. Various other grids are used for the other Ocean Wave types. The grids for the larger quilts (Full/Queen Quilt, Twin Coverlet and Wall Quilt) are marked in 3⅜" squares to make 2½" finished triangle-squares. The grids for the small quilts (Doll Quilt, Mini Wall Quilt) are marked in 1⅞" squares to make one-inch finished triangle-squares.

Grid-Method Quick-Piecing for Multi-Fabric Ocean Waves (Random-Scrap, Scrap-With-Constant, Wedge)

Marking

Place the two fabric pieces right sides together. Pressing the two-fabric combination before marking helps "marry" the two fabrics so they won't slip during marking and sewing.

Use a pencil to mark the grid exactly as shown, coming in a bit from the edges of the fabric to mark.

If you are marking the Full/Queen Quilt, Twin Coverlet or Wall quilt, mark Grid #1 on 9" x 22" fabric pieces. Each square of the grid must be 3⅜".

If you are making the Doll Quilt or Mini Wall Quilt, mark Grid #1 on 5½" x 13" pieces of fabric. Each square of the grid must be 1⅞".

The lines shown on the Grid #1 diagram will be cutting lines. Notice that only one diagonal line goes through each square. Omit the diagonal marks in the two far right squares. These squares are left unsewn, and will produce single triangles needed for making Ocean Waves units. You can pin the combination together in a few places if you wish. See the Box on page 14 for a way to speed up the marking process.

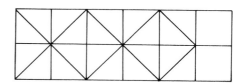

Grid #1
6 x 2 squares
Produces 20 ◨
8 ◺

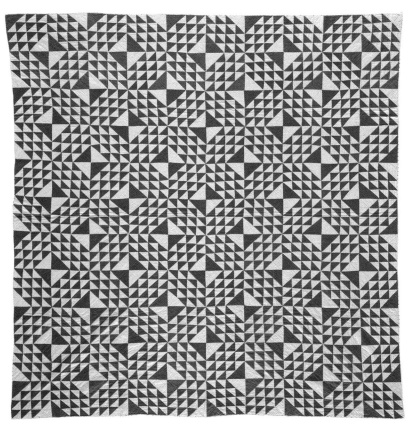

◄ **2** The fabrics that appear to be white in this circa 1890 Ocean Waves are actually a variety of tiny "shirting prints." We named this Ocean Waves variation "Split-Set" because the setting pieces are split into triangles. (Ocean Waves 70″ x 75″, collection of Liz Porter.)

▼ **3** Amish quiltmakers have often made Ocean Waves quilts, primarily in rural, rather than seaside communities. This vibrant example with Sawtooth border was made around 1935 in Holmes County, Ohio. (Ocean Waves, 68″ x 66″, Esprit Quilt Collection, San Francisco. Photograph by Sharon Risedorph.)

7 Mary Lou Jones of Des Moines selected sixty different pink prints for her Full/Queen Random-Scrap Ocean Waves, ranging from baby pink to deep burgundy. The setting pieces are also a pink print. The cable circle quilting pattern for the setting pieces is on page 61. (Random-Scrap Ocean Waves, 80″ x 100″, 1988, Mary Lou Jones).

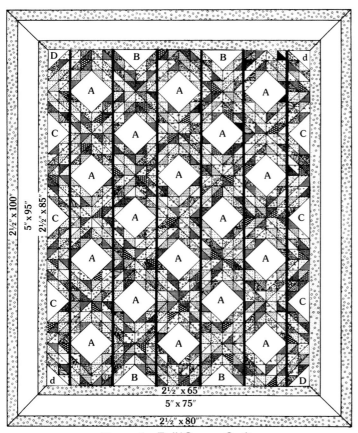

Figure 1, Full/Queen Quilt.

Twin Coverlet 60" x 80"

I. Cut Borders and Setting Pieces.
From Fabric #1, cut: 2 middle borders, 5½" x 78"
                      2 middle borders, 5½" x 58"

                      setting pieces, 8 A squares
                              6 BC triangles
                              4 D triangles

From Fabric #2, cut: 2 outer borders, 3" x 83"
                      2 inner borders, 3" x 68"
                      2 outer borders, 3" x 63"
                      2 inner borders, 3" x 48"

II. Make Quick-Pieced Triangle-Squares.
Using the quick-piecing technique for 2½" finished triangle-squares, pair your 30 fabrics with each other to make 15 combinations for quick piecing. Use Grid #1 for your marking pattern, marking a grid of 3⅜" squares.

The Grid #1 arrangement makes 20 triangle-squares and eight single triangles per combination, a total of 300 triangle-squares and 120 single triangles. The Twin Coverlet requires 240 triangle-squares and 96 single triangles, so you will have leftovers.

III. Construct Ocean Waves Units.
Refer to the Unit Chart and combine triangle-squares, single triangles and setting pieces to make the units needed for the Twin Coverlet.

IV. Set the Quilt Top.
Sew A-d units together in five vertical rows as shown in Figure 2. Sew the rows together to form the quilt top.

V.
Follow instruction V for the Full/Queen Quilt to complete the Twin Coverlet.

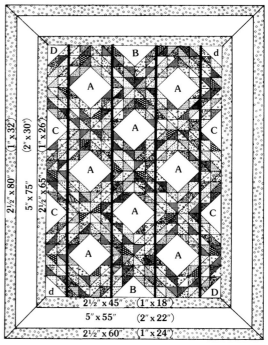

Figure 2, Twin Coverlet. (Measurements in parentheses are for Doll Quilt.)

Doll Quilt 24" x 32"

I. Cut Borders and Setting Pieces.
From Fabric #1, cut: 2 middle borders, 2½" x 33"
                      2 middle borders, 2½" x 25"

                      setting pieces, 8 A squares
                              6 BC triangles
                              4 D triangles

From Fabric #2, cut: 2 outer borders, 1½" x 35"
2 inner borders, 1½" x 29"
2 outer borders, 1½" x 27"
2 inner borders, 1½" x 21"

II. Make Quick-Pieced Triangle-Squares. Using the quick-piecing technique for one-inch finished triangle-squares, pair your 30 fabrics with each other to make 15 combinations for quick piecing. Use Grid #1 for your marking pattern, marking a grid of 1⅞" squares.

The Grid #1 arrangement makes 20 triangle-squares and eight single triangles per combination, a total of 300 triangle-squares and 120 single triangles. The Doll Quilt requires 240 triangle-squares and 96 single triangles, so you will have leftovers.

III. Follow instructions III through V for the Twin Coverlet to complete the Doll Quilt.

Wall Quilt 50" x 50"

I. Cut Borders and Setting Pieces.
From Fabric #1, cut: setting pieces, 5 A squares
4 BC triangles
4 D triangles

From Fabric #2, cut: 4 borders, 5½" x 53"

II. Make Quick-Pieced Triangle-Squares. Using the quick-piecing technique for 2½" finished triangle-squares, pair your 24 fabrics with each other to make 12 combinations for quick piecing. Use Grid #1 for your marking pattern, making a grid of 3⅜" squares.

The Grid #1 arrangement makes 20 triangle-squares and eight single triangles per combination, a total of 240 triangle-squares and 96 single triangles. The Wall Quilt requires 160 triangle-squares and 64 single triangles, so you will have leftovers.

III. Construct Ocean Waves Units. Refer to the Unit Chart and combine triangle-squares, single triangles and setting pieces to make the units needed for the Wall Quilt.

IV. Set the Quilt Top. Sew A-d units together in five vertical rows as shown in Figure 3. Sew the rows together to form the quilt top.

V. Add the Borders. Center and sew a border to each side of the quilt top. See General Instructions for tips on adding and mitering borders.

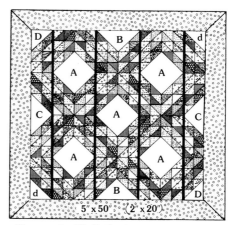

Figure 3, Wall Quilt. (Measurements in parentheses are for Mini Wall Quilt.)

Mini Wall Quilt 20" x 20"

I. Cut Borders and Setting Pieces.
From Fabric #1, cut: setting pieces, 5 A squares
4 BC triangles
4 D triangles

From Fabric #2, cut: 4 borders, 2½" x 23"

II. Make Quick-Pieced Triangle-Squares. Using the quick-piecing technique for one-inch finished triangle-squares described in the General Instructions section of this book, pair your 24 fabrics with each other to make 12 combinations for quick piecing. Use Grid #1 for your marking pattern, marking a grid of 1⅞" squares.

The Grid #1 arrangement makes 20 triangle-squares and eight single triangles per combination, a total of 240 triangle-squares and 96 single triangles. The Mini Wall Quilt requires 160 triangle-squares and 64 single triangles, so you will have leftovers.

III. Follow Instructions III through V for the Wall Quilt to complete the Mini Wall Quilt.

8   Authors Fons and Porter made this, their first Ocean Waves quilt, for a 1985 issue of *Creative Ideas for Living* magazine. Each of the women supplied half of the over 60 scrap fabrics for the triangle-squares. Many of the fabrics used, they claim, are quite ugly, but they all work well together in totally random placement. The feather quilting design is on page 63. (Random-Scrap Ocean Waves, 80″ x 100″, 1984, Marianne Fons and Liz Porter, quilted by Helen Martens.)

9   So they could each have a full-size Ocean Waves quilt to keep, authors Fons and Porter made their second Random-Scrap version soon after the first. They used 30 pink and 30 blue prints for the triangle-squares and admit they did so without having to buy any! Both the pinks and the blues range from the pastel "baby" shades to quite dark ones. The clamshell quilting pattern is on page 62. (Random-Scrap Ocean Waves, 80″ x 100″, Marianne Fons and Liz Porter, quilted in 1988 by Evalee Waltz.)

Scrap-with-Constant Ocean Waves

The Scrap-With-Constant Ocean Waves quilts in this book use 12 to 30 different fabrics that are always combined with a constant fabric to make the triangle-squares. Fifteen different pastel solids were paired with ivory each time to make the triangles for the Full/Queen Quilt on the cover, also shown on page 32. The Wall Quilt in Photo 12 has various pinks and blues combined with muslin. Amish solids were used with black solid as the constant fabric for the Wall Quilt in Photo 12 and the Twin Coverlet in Photo 13.

Borders and Setting Pieces

The Scrap-With-Constant quilts in this book each have a middle sawtooth border with fabric borders to each side.

The cutting measurements for fabric borders include ¼" seam allowances. Borders are first cut a few inches longer than needed. The borders will be trimmed to exact length when added to quilt top. Refer to pages 18–19 for instructions on marking and cutting the setting pieces.

Yardages for Scrap-With-Constant Ocean Waves

Yardages are for 44"–45" wide fabric.

Full/Queen Quilt 75" x 95"

7¾ yards Fabric #1 for triangles, setting pieces and borders

¼ yard each (9" x 44" pieces) of 15 different fabrics for triangles, or ⅛ yard each (9" x 22" pieces) of 30 different fabrics

¾ yard fabric for binding   6 yards for backing

Twin Coverlet 55" x 75"

4¾ yards Fabric #1 for triangles, setting pieces and borders

⅛ yard each (9" x 22" pieces) of 17 different fabrics for triangles

¾ yard fabric for binding   5 yards for backing

Doll Quilt 22" x 30"

1¾ yards Fabric #1 for triangles, setting pieces and borders

Scraps (5½" x 13") of 17 different fabrics for triangles

¼ yard fabric for binding   1 yard for backing

Wall Quilt 55" x 55"

3½ yards Fabric #1 for triangles, setting pieces and borders

⅛ yard each (9" x 22" pieces) of 12 different fabrics for triangles

½ yard fabric for binding   3½ yards for backing

Mini Wall Quilt 22" x 22"

1¼ yards Fabric #1 for triangles, setting pieces and borders

Scraps (5½" x 13") of 12 different fabrics for triangles

¼ yard fabric for binding   1 yard for backing

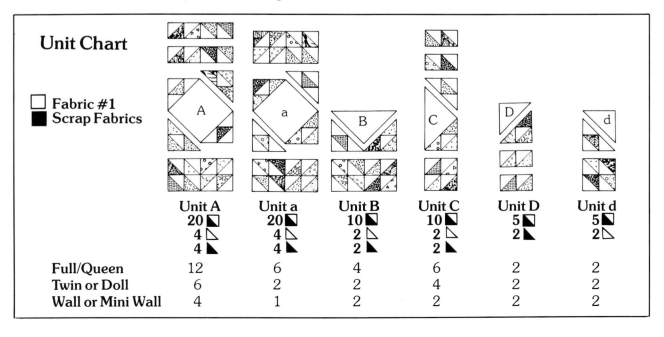

Unit Chart

☐ Fabric #1
■ Scrap Fabrics

	Unit A	Unit a	Unit B	Unit C	Unit D	Unit d
	20 ◩	20 ◩	10 ◩	10 ◩	5 ◩	5 ◩
	4 ◹	4 ◹	2 ◹	2 ◹	2 ◥	2 ◹
	4 ◣	4 ◣	2 ◣	2 ◣		2 ◣
Full/Queen	12	6	4	6	2	2
Twin or Doll	6	2	2	4	2	2
Wall or Mini Wall	4	1	2	2	2	2

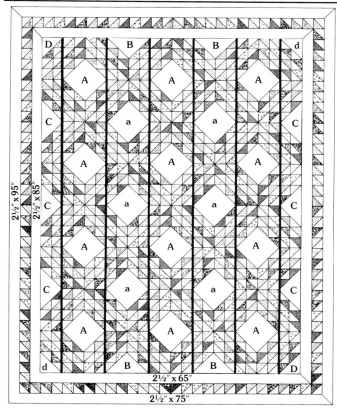

Figure 1, Full/Queen Quilt.

Full/Queen Quilt 75" x 95"

I. Cut Borders and Setting Pieces.

From Fabric #1, cut: 2 outer borders, 3" x 98"
2 inner borders, 3" x 88"
2 outer borders, 3" x 78"
2 inner borders, 3" x 68"
setting pieces, 18 A squares
10 BC triangles
4 D triangles

II. Make Quick-Pieced Triangle-Squares.
Cut or tear thirty 9" x 22" pieces of Fabric #1. Cut each ¼ yard scrap fabric into two 9" x 22" pieces (30 pieces total). Using the quick-piecing technique for 2½" finished triangle-squares, pair the 30 fabric pieces with the pieces of Fabric #1. Use Grid #1 for your marking pattern, marking a grid of 3⅜" squares.

This grid arrangement makes 20 triangle-squares and eight single triangles per combination, a total of 600 triangle-squares and 240 singles. The Full/Queen Quilt requires 604 triangle-squares (480 for inner quilt, 124 for sawtooth border), and 192 single triangles. Combine eight of the leftover single triangles to make four more triangle-squares.

III. Construct Ocean Waves Quilt Units.
Refer to the Unit Chart and combine triangle-squares, single triangles and setting pieces to make the units needed for the Full/Queen Quilt. See the Box on page 20 for hints on sewing and pressing Ocean Waves units.

IV. Set the Quilt Top.
Sew A-d units together in seven vertical rows as shown in Figure 1. Sew the rows together to form the quilt top.

V. Add the Borders.
Refer to the quilt diagram (Figure 1) and combine remaining triangle-squares to form the sawtooth border. The sides use 34 triangle-squares each, the ends 28 each.

Add fabric and pieced borders to quilt top. See General Instructions for tips on adding borders.

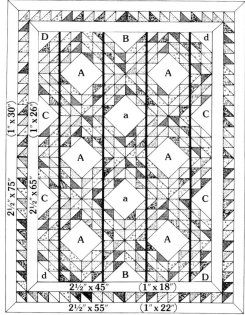

Figure 2, Twin Coverlet. (Measurements in parentheses are for Doll Quilt.)

Twin Coverlet 55" x 75"

I. Cut Borders and Setting Pieces.

From Fabric #1, cut: 2 outer borders, 3" x 78"
2 inner borders, 3" x 68"
2 outer borders, 3" x 58"
2 inner borders, 3" x 48"
setting pieces, 8 A squares
6 BC triangles
4 D triangles

II. Make Quick-Pieced Triangle-Squares.
Cut or tear seventeen 9" x 22" pieces of Fabric #1. Using the quick-piecing technique for 2½" finished triangle-squares, pair the 17 scrap fabric pieces with the pieces of Fabric #1. Use Grid #1 for your marking pattern, marking a grid of 3⅜" squares.

This grid arrangement makes 20 triangle-squares and eight single triangles per combination, a total of 340 triangle-squares and 136 singles. The Twin Coverlet requires 332 triangle-squares (240 for inner quilt, 92 for sawtooth border), and 96 single triangles.

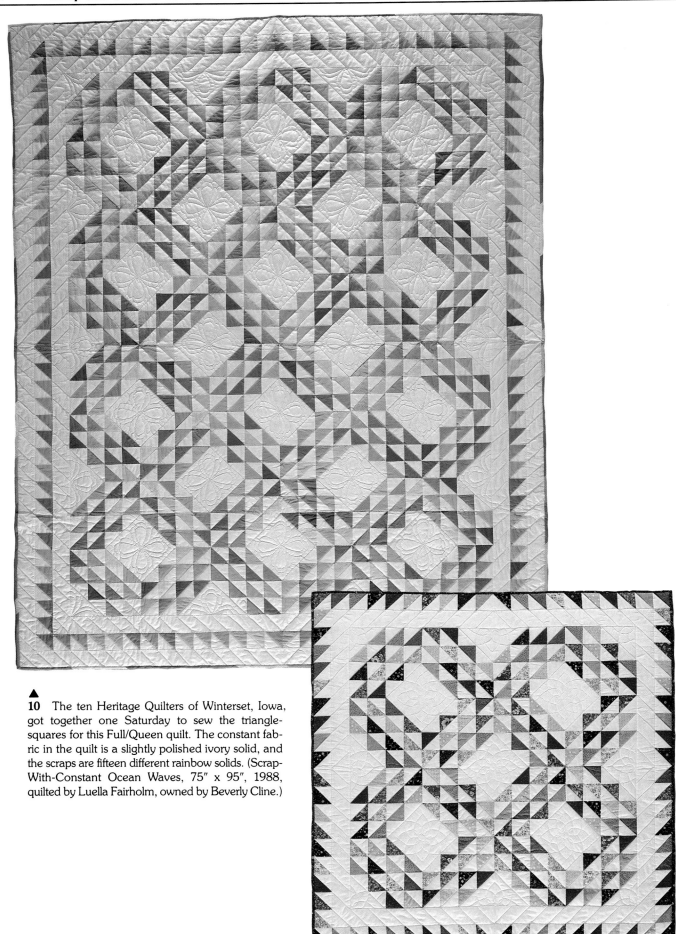

▲
10 The ten Heritage Quilters of Winterset, Iowa, got together one Saturday to sew the triangle-squares for this Full/Queen quilt. The constant fabric in the quilt is a slightly polished ivory solid, and the scraps are fifteen different rainbow solids. (Scrap-With-Constant Ocean Waves, 75″ x 95″, 1988, quilted by Luella Fairholm, owned by Beverly Cline.)

13 Martha Meyer started this Twin Coverlet in an Ocean Waves workshop by Marianne Fons. A confirmed night-owl and non-stop sewer, Martha finished piecing and machine-quilting her project in less than a month. She was inspired by her desire to present the quilt to her step-son as a graduation gift. Martha used black as her constant fabric, combining it with various bright solids for the triangle-squares. (Scrap-With-Constant Ocean Waves, 55" x 75", 1988, Martha Meyer.)

◄ ▶
11, 12 Both these Wall Quilts got underway in a Madison, Wisconsin, workshop. Joan Stuesser used muslin as her constant, combining it with twelve different pink and blue scrap fabrics. Sylvia Lewis combined twelve Amish solids with black for her wall quilt. Both women used a combination of hand and machine quilting. Note that Wall Quilt instructions in this book are for two narrow fabric borders with the Sawtooth border between. Joan used just one muslin border, ending her quilt with the Sawtooth piecing. Sylvia used no pieced border, just a narrow solid blue and then a wider black border. (Scrap-With-Constant Ocean Waves, 50" x 50", 1988, Joan Stuesser, Scrap-With-Constant Ocean Waves, 55" x 55", 1988, Sylvia Lewis.)

III. Construct Ocean Waves Quilt Units. Refer to the Unit Chart and combine triangle-squares, single triangles and setting pieces to make the units needed for the Twin Coverlet.

IV. Set the Quilt Top. Sew A-d units together in five vertical rows as shown in Figure 2. Sew the rows together to form the quilt top.

V. Add the Borders. Refer to Figure 2 and combine remaining triangle-squares to form the sawtooth border. The sides use 26 triangle-squares each, the ends 20 each. Add fabric and pieced borders to quilt top.

Doll Quilt 22" x 30"

I. Cut Borders and Setting Pieces.
From Fabric #1, cut: 2 outer borders, 1½" x 32"
2 inner borders, 1½" x 28"
2 outer borders, 1½" x 24"
2 inner borders, 1½" x 20"
setting pieces, 8 A squares
6 BC triangles
4 D triangles

II. Make Quick-Pieced Triangle-Squares. Cut or tear seventeen 5½" x 13" pieces of Fabric #1. Using the quick-piecing technique for one-inch finished triangle-squares, pair the 17 scrap fabric pieces with the pieces of Fabric #1. Use Grid #1 for your marking pattern, marking a grid of 1⅞" squares.

This grid arrangement makes 20 triangle-squares and eight single triangles per combination, a total of 340 triangle-squares and 136 singles. The Doll Quilt requires 332 triangle-squares (240 for inner quilt, 92 for sawtooth border), and 96 single triangles.

III. Follow instructions III through V for Twin Coverlet to complete Doll Quilt.

Wall Quilt 55" x 55"

I. Cut Borders and Setting Pieces.
From Fabric #1, cut: 4 outer borders, 3" x 58"
4 inner borders, 3" x 48"
setting pieces, 5 A squares
4 BC triangles
4 D triangles

II. Make Quick-Pieced Triangle-Squares. Cut or tear twelve 9" x 22" pieces of Fabric #1. Using the quick-piecing technique for 2½" finished triangle-squares, pair the twelve scrap fabric pieces with the pieces of Fabric #1. Use Grid #1 for your marking pattern, marking a grid of 3⅜" squares.

This grid arrangement makes 20 triangle-squares and eight single triangles per combination, a total of 240 triangle-squares and 96 singles. The Wall Quilt requires 236 triangle-squares (160 for inner quilt, 76 for sawtooth border), and 64 single triangles.

III. Construct Ocean Waves Quilt Units. Refer to the Unit Chart and combine triangle-squares, single triangles and setting pieces to make the A-d units needed for the Wall Quilt.

IV. Set the Quilt Top. Sew A-d units together in five vertical rows as shown in Figure 3. Sew the rows together to form the quilt top.

V. Add the Borders. Refer to Figure 3 and combine remaining triangle-squares to form the sawtooth border. The sides use 18 triangle-squares each, the top and bottom 20 each.

Figure 3, Wall Quilt. (Measurements in parentheses are for Mini Wall Quilt.)

Mini Wall Quilt 22" x 22"
I. Cut Borders and Setting Pieces.
From Fabric #1, cut: 4 outer borders, 1½" x 24"
4 inner borders, 1½" x 20"
setting pieces, 5 A squares
4 BC triangles
4 D triangles

II. Make Quick-Pieced Triangle-Squares. Cut or tear twelve 5½" x 13" pieces of Fabric #1. Using the quick-piecing technique for one-inch finished triangle-squares, pair the twelve scrap pieces with the pieces of Fabric #1. Use Grid #1 for your marking pattern, marking a grid of 1⅞" squares.

This grid arrangement makes 20 triangle-squares and eight single triangles per combination, a total of 240 triangle-squares and 96 singles. The Mini Wall Quilt requires a 236 triangle-squares (160 for inner quilt, 76 for sawtooth border), and 64 single triangles.

III. Follow instructions III through V for Wall Quilt to complete Mini Wall Quilt.

Wedge Ocean Waves

The Wedge Style Ocean Waves variation is made of a number of different prints or solids used with a constant fabric. Each of the various fabrics is combined with the constant fabric to make the triangle-squares for the quilt. Then the same-fabric triangle-squares are positioned in wedge-shaped arrangements in the quilt.

The Full/Queen size quilt in this book is designed to use 24 different fabrics with the single constant. The smaller quilts use fewer fabrics. The Wedge Twin Coverlet in Photo 14 uses four pink, four blue and four purple prints for its twelve fabrics. Antique fabrics were combined for the Doll Quilt in Photo 16. The Wall Quilt in Photo 15 combines Amish solid colors for its wedges.

Borders and Setting Pieces

For borders, two strips of the constant fabric are separated by a narrower border pieced of random lengths of some of the various other fabrics used for the triangles, with the exception of the two Wall Quilts, which just have a single fabric border.

The cutting measurements for fabric borders include ¼″ seam allowances. The borders are first cut longer than needed and trimmed to length when added to the quilt top. Refer to pages 18−19 for instructions on marking and cutting setting pieces.

Yardages for Wedge Style Ocean Waves

Yardages are for 44″−45″ fabric.

Full/Queen Quilt 79″ x 99″

(24 different fabrics combined with a constant fabric)

7 yards of Fabric #1 (constant) for inner and outer borders, setting pieces and triangles

¼ yard each (9″ x 44″ pieces) of 24 different fabrics for triangles and middle borders

¾ yard fabric for binding   6 yards for backing

Twin Coverlet 59″ x 79″

(12 different fabrics combined with a constant fabric)

4¾ yards of Fabric #1 (constant) for inner and outer borders, setting pieces and triangles

¼ yard each (9″ x 44″ pieces) of 12 different fabrics for middle borders and triangles

¾ yard fabric for binding   5 yards for backing

Doll Quilt 25½″ x 33½″

(12 different fabrics combined with a constant fabric)

1¾ yards of Fabric #1 (constant) for inner and outer borders, setting pieces and triangles

Scraps, (7″ x 13″) of 12 different fabrics for middle borders and triangles

¼ yard fabric for binding   1 yard for backing

Wall Quilt 46″ x 46″

(8 different fabrics combined with a constant fabric)

2¾ yards Fabric #1 (constant) for inner and outer borders, setting pieces and triangles

¼ yard each of 8 different fabrics (9″ x 44″ pieces) for middle borders and triangles

¼ yard fabric for binding   3½ yards for backing

Mini Wall Quilt 20″ x 20″

(8 different fabrics combined with a constant fabric)

1¼ yards Fabric #1 (constant) for borders, setting pieces and triangles

Scraps (5½″ x 13″) of 8 different fabrics for triangles

¼ yard fabric for binding   1 yard for backing

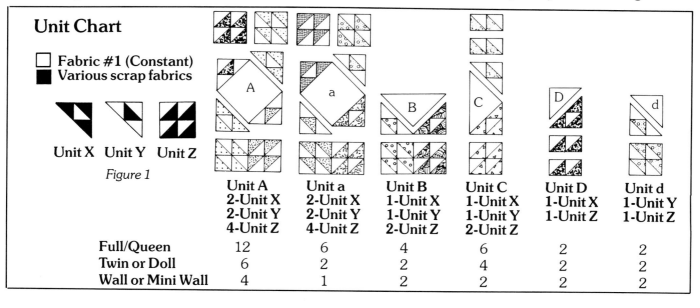

Unit Chart

☐ Fabric #1 (Constant)
■ Various scrap fabrics

Unit X   Unit Y   Unit Z

Figure 1

	Unit A 2-Unit X 2-Unit Y 4-Unit Z	Unit a 2-Unit X 2-Unit Y 4-Unit Z	Unit B 1-Unit X 1-Unit Y 2-Unit Z	Unit C 1-Unit X 1-Unit Y 2-Unit Z	Unit D 1-Unit X 1-Unit Z	Unit d 1-Unit Y 1-Unit Z
Full/Queen	12	6	4	6	2	2
Twin or Doll	6	2	2	4	2	2
Wall or Mini Wall	4	1	2	2	2	2

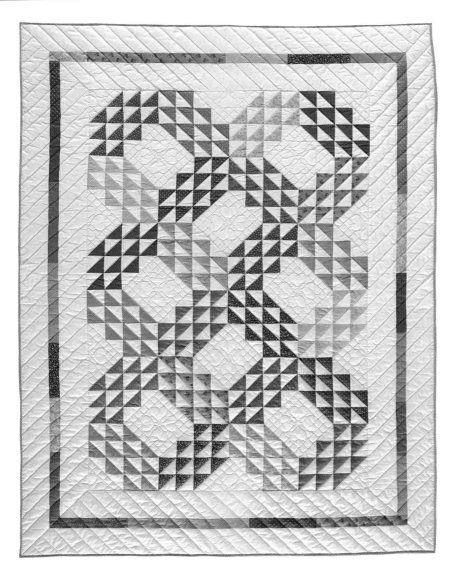

14 Working each evening in their hotel room until after midnight, authors Fons and Porter machine-pieced this Twin Coverlet while at a week-long quilt conference. The quilt uses four pink, four purple and four blue prints for the wedges, with each print making two wedge sections. The middle border is made of random-length strips of the wedge fabrics. (Wedge Ocean Waves, 59″ x 79″, 1988. Marianne Fons and Liz Porter, quilted by Betty Means.)

15 Sally Cameron of Madison, Wisconsin, used a rainbow of greyed solids with black in her Wall Quilt, which she named "Waves on the Horizon." Her quilt is really a Wedge variation, since some of the wedge-shaped sections have more than one shade of fabric in them. Sally's careful grading of color gives the quilt its prismatic quality. (Wedge Ocean Waves, 47″ x 47″, 1988, Sally Cameron.)

16 A small collection of antique indigo prints was skillfully combined with muslin by Donna Brayman of rural Winterset to make this charming old-fashioned Wedge Doll Quilt. The yardage requirements for the Doll Quilt call for twelve different scrap fabrics, enough for two wedges of each fabric. But if you're using old fabrics, you may have to mete them out carefully, as Donna did, using a different fabric for each wedge. In fact, Donna even used more than one fabric in one of the wedges, giving the quilt a true nineteenth-century character. (Wedge Ocean Waves, 25 ½" x 33 ½", 1988, Donna Brayman.)

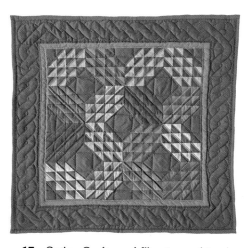

17 Cathy Grafton of Illinois combined eight greyed-down Amish solids with a dull brown-purple to give this Mini Wall Quilt a really antique look. Each of the eight fabrics is used in two wedges. Instead of a single two-inch fabric border as described in the instructions, Kathy varied her project by adding three-fourths-inch-wide and three-inch-wide fabric borders. (Wedge Ocean Waves, 26" x 26", 1988, Cathy Grafton.)

Full/Queen Quilt 79" x 99"

I. Cut Borders and Setting Pieces.
From Fabric #1, cut: 2 outer borders, 4½" x 95"
2 inner borders, 4½" x 84"
2 outer borders, 4½" x 83"
2 inner borders, 4½" x 72"
setting pieces, 18 A squares
10 BC triangles
4 D triangles

II. Make Quick-Pieced Triangle-Squares. Cut or tear a 9" x 22" piece from each of the 24 quarter-yard pieces. Using the quick-piecing technique for 2½" finished triangle-squares described in the General Instructions section of this book, pair the twenty-four 9" x 22" pieces with 9" x 22" pieces of Fabric #1. (The leftover pieces of the 24 fabrics will be used in the middle border.)

Use Grid #1 for your marking pattern, marking a grid of 3⅜" squares. The Grid #1 arrangement makes 20 triangle-squares and eight single triangles per combination, a total of 480 triangle-squares and 192 singles. This is the exact number of triangle-squares and single triangles needed for the Full/Queen Quilt.

III. Sew Wedge Units. Referring to Figure 1 in the Unit Chart, make two each of wedge units X and Y and four of wedge unit Z from each of the 24 fabric combinations. Press the seam allowances away from the triangle-squares when making the X and Y units.

IV. Construct Ocean Waves Quilt Units. Referring to Figure 2, lay out the setting pieces and X, Y and Z wedge units, placing the X, Y, and Z units so they form wedges of the same fabric.

Refer to the Unit Chart and combine the setting pieces and X, Y and Z wedge units to form the Ocean Waves units needed for the Full/Queen quilt.

V. Set the Quilt Top. Sew Ocean Waves units together in seven vertical rows as shown in Figure 2. Sew the rows together to form the quilt top.

VI. Add the Borders. The middle borders are pieced from random length 2" wide (1½" finished) segments of the 24 fabrics used in the quilt top.

Cut random-length 2"-wide segments of the 24 fabrics. Piece the segments into two borders, each approximately 73" long, for the top and bottom of the quilt, and two borders, each approximately 91" long, for the sides of the quilt.

Refer to Figure 2 and add inner, middle and outer borders to quilt top.

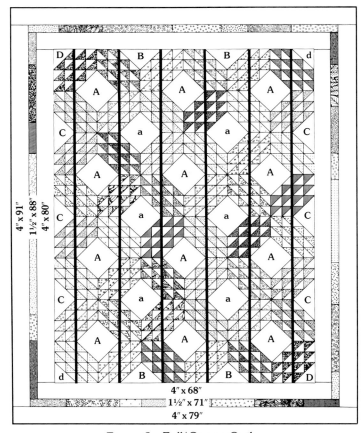

Figure 2, Full/Queen Quilt.

Twin Coverlet 59" x 79"

I. Cut Borders and Setting Pieces.

From Fabric #1, cut: 2 outer borders, 4½" x 74"
2 inner borders, 4½" x 63"
2 outer borders, 4½" x 63"
2 inner borders, 4½" x 52"
setting pieces, 8 A squares
6 BC triangles
4 D triangles

II. Make Quick-Pieced Triangle-Squares. Cut or
tear a 9" x 22" piece from each of the 12 quarter-yard
pieces. Using the quick-piecing technique for 2½"
finished triangle-squares, pair the twelve 9" x 22"
pieces with 9" x 22" pieces of Fabric #1. (The left-
over pieces of the 12 fabrics will be used in the middle border.)

Use Grid #1 for your marking pattern, marking a
grid of 3⅜" squares. The Grid #1 arrangement
makes 20 triangle-squares and eight single triangles
per combination, a total of 240 triangle-squares and
96 singles. This is the exact number of triangle-
squares and single triangles needed for the Twin
Coverlet.

III. Sew Wedge Units. Referring to Figure 1 on the
Unit Chart, make two each of wedge units X and Y
and four of wedge unit Z from each of the 12 fabric
combinations.

IV. Construct the Ocean Waves Units. Referring to
Figure 3, lay out the setting pieces and X, Y and Z
wedge units so they form wedges of the same fabric.

Refer to the Unit Chart and combine the setting
pieces, and X, Y and Z wedge units to form the
Ocean Waves units needed for your quilt.

V. Add the Borders. The middle borders are pieced
from random lengths 2" wide (1½" finished) segments of the 12 fabrics used in the quilt top.

Cut random-length 2" wide segments from the 12
fabrics. Piece segments into two borders, each approximately 54" long, for the top and bottom borders, and two borders, each approximately 71" long,
for the side borders. Refer to Figure 3 and add inner,
middle and outer borders to quilt top.

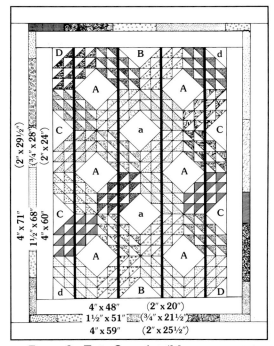

*Figure 3, Twin Coverlet. (Measurements in
parentheses are for Mini Wall Quilt.)*

Doll Quilt 25½" x 33½"

I. Cut Borders and Setting Pieces.

From Fabric #1, cut: 2 outer borders, 2½" x 33"
2 outer borders, 2½" x 29"
2 inner borders, 2½" x 27"
2 inner borders, 2½" x 23"
setting pieces, 8 A squares
6 BC triangles
4 D triangles

From each of the 12 different fabrics, cut:
1 strip, 1¼" wide x 13" for
segments of middle border

II. Make Quick-Pieced Triangle-Squares. Using the quick-piecing technique for one-inch finished triangle-squares described in the General Instructions section of this book, pair the 12 scrap fabric pieces with 5½" x 13" pieces of Fabric #1.

Use Grid #1 for your marking pattern, marking a grid of 1⅞" squares. The Grid #1 arrangement makes 20 triangle-squares and eight single triangles per combination, a total of 240 triangle-squares and 96 singles. This is the exact number of triangle-squares and single triangles needed for the Doll Quilt.

III. Follow instructions III and IV for Twin Coverlet.

V. Add the Borders. The middle borders are pieced from random length 1¼" wide (¾" finished) segments of the 12 fabrics used for the quilt top.

Trim border segments to random lengths. Piece segments into two borders, each approximately 24" long, for the top and bottom of the quilt, and two borders, each approximately 31" long, for the sides. Refer to Figure 3 and add inner, middle and outer borders.

Wall Quilt 47" x 47"

I. Cut Borders and Setting Pieces.
From Fabric #1, cut: 4 borders, 4" x 50"
setting pieces, 5 A squares
4 BC triangles
4 D triangles

II. Make Quick-Pieced Triangle-Squares. Cut or tear a 9" x 22" piece from each of the eight quarter-yard pieces. Using the quick-piecing technique for 2½" finished triangle-squares, pair the eight 9" x 22" pieces with 9" x 22" pieces of Fabric #1. (The left-over pieces of the fabrics will be used in the middle border.)

Use Grid #1 for your marking pattern, marking a grid of 3⅜" squares. The Grid #1 arrangement makes 20 triangle-squares and eight single triangles per combination, a total of 160 triangle-squares and 64 singles. This is the exact number of triangle-squares and single triangles needed for the Wall Quilt.

III. Sew Wedge Units. Referring to Figure 1 on the Unit Chart, make two each of the wedge units X and Y and four of wedge unit Z from each of the eight fabric combinations.

IV. Construct the Ocean Waves Quilt Units. Referring to Figure 4, lay out the setting pieces and X, Y, and Z wedge units so they form wedges of the same fabric. Refer to the Unit Chart and combine the setting pieces and X, Y, and Z wedge units to form the Ocean Waves units needed for your quilt.

V. Set the Quilt Top. Sew Ocean Waves units together in five vertical rows as shown in Figure 4. Sew the rows together to form the inner quilt top.

VI. Add the Borders. Center and stitch a border to each side of the quilt top. Miter the border corner seams. See General Instructions on mitering corners.

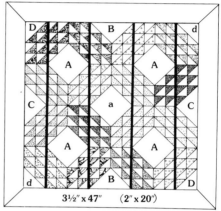

3½" x 47"   (2" x 20")

Figure 4, Wall Quilt. (Measurements parentheses are for Mini Wall Quilt.)

Mini Wall Quilt 20" x 20"

I. Cut Borders and Setting Pieces.
From Fabric #1, cut: 4 borders, 2½" x 23"
setting pieces, 5 A squares
4 BC triangles
4 D triangles

II. Make Quick-Pieced Triangle-Squares. Using the quick-piecing technique for one-inch finished triangle-squares described in the General Instructions section of this book, pair the eight scrap pieces with 5½" x 13" pieces of Fabric #1.

Use Grid #1 for your marking pattern, marking a grid of 1⅞" squares. The Grid #1 arrangement makes 20 triangle-squares and eight single triangles per combination, a total of 160 triangle-squares and 64 singles. This is the exact number of triangle-squares and single triangles needed for the Wall Quilt.

III. Follow instructions III through VI for the Wall Quilt to complete Mini Wall Quilt.

18 Iowans Mary Miller and Marilyn Parks worked as a team to produce this twin coverlet, which is machine-pieced and both hand and machine-quilted. They used a large-scale lilac print for the setting pieces and half the triangles, combining it with a solid lilac. The partners still aren't sure who owns the quilt. (Two-Fabric Ocean Waves, 60" x 80", 1988, Mary Miller and Marilyn Parks.)

19, 20 These two Mini-Wall Quilts have the same dimensions but quite different fabric treatments. Jackie Leckband of Iowa used two old-fashioned prints, a dark green and a pink check. Marianne Fons combined two tiny prints, one a red print with little stars and the other a confetti-like natural print. Both quilts have a zig-zag border as shown in the quilt instructions. (Two-Fabric Ocean Waves, 24" x 24", 1988, Jackie Leckband. Two-Fabric Ocean Waves, 24" x 24", 1988, Marianne Fons.)

Two-Fabric Ocean Waves

As its name indicates, the Two-Fabric Ocean Waves variation uses two fabrics only for all the pieces. The Twin Coverlet in Photo 18 combines a paisley print with solid lilac. The Mini Wall Quilt in Photo 19 has the look of an antique quilt but is made of new fabrics. Another Mini Wall Quilt, Photo 20, is made of two small scale prints.

Borders and Setting Pieces

All the Two-Fabric Ocean Waves quilts in this book have a zig-zag middle border with a fabric border to each side. The cutting measurements for borders include ¼″ seam allowances. Borders are first cut a few inches longer than needed. The borders will be trimmed to exact length when added to the quilt top. Refer to pages 18–19 for instructions on marking and cutting the setting pieces.

Yardages for Two-Fabric Style Ocean Waves

Yardages are for 44″–45″ wide fabric.

Full/Queen Quilt 80″ x 100″

6½ yards Fabric #1 for triangles and borders

6½ yards Fabric #2 for triangles and setting pieces

¾ yard fabric for binding   6 yards for backing

Twin Coverlet 60″ x 80″

4½ yards Fabric #1 for triangles and borders

3½ yards Fabric #2 for triangles and setting pieces

¾ yard fabric for binding   5 yards for backing

Doll Quilt 24″ x 32″

1½ yard Fabric #1 for triangles and borders

1½ yard Fabric #2 for triangles and setting pieces

¼ yard fabric for binding   1 yard for backing

Wall Quilt 60″ x 60″

3¾ yards Fabric #1 for triangles and borders

2½ yards Fabric #2 for triangles and setting pieces

½ yard fabric for binding   3½ yards for backing

Mini Wall Quilt 24″ x 24″

1¼ yard Fabric #1 for triangles and borders

1¼ yard Fabric #2 for triangles and setting pieces

¼ yard binding fabric   1 yard for backing

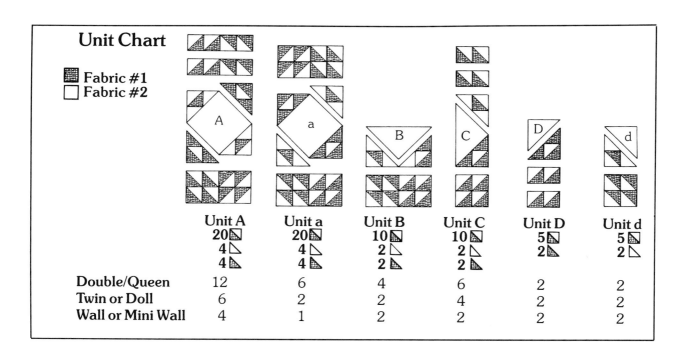

	Unit A	Unit a	Unit B	Unit C	Unit D	Unit d
	20	20	10	10	5	5
	4	4	2	2	2	2
	4	4	2	2		
Double/Queen	12	6	4	6	2	2
Twin or Doll	6	2	2	4	2	2
Wall or Mini Wall	4	1	2	2	2	2

Unit Chart

Fabric #1
Fabric #2

Full/Queen Quilt 80" x 100"

I. Cut Borders and Setting Pieces.
From Fabric #1, cut: 2 outer borders, 3" x 103"
2 inner borders, 3" x 88"
2 outer borders, 3" x 83"
2 inner borders, 3" x 68"

From Fabric #2, cut: setting pieces, 18 A squares
10 BC triangles
4 triangles

II. Make Quick-Pieced Triangle-Squares. From remaining Fabric #1 and Fabric #2, cut or tear twelve 18" x 22" pieces of each fabric.

Refer to the General Instructions section of this book and combine the fabric pieces to make 2½" finished triangle-squares. Use Grid #9 for your marking pattern, marking a grid of 3⅜" squares.

This grid arrangement makes 60 triangle-squares per combination, a total of 720 triangle-squares, once all twelve combinations are sewn.

The Full/Queen Quilt requires a total of 736 triangle squares (480 of them for the inner quilt and 256 for the zig-zag border), so you need 16 more triangle-squares. To make the additional triangle-squares, you will need a 9" x 19" piece of each fabric. Pair, mark and sew, using Grid #4 for your marking pattern. This grid arrangement produces 20 triangle-squares, which will provide a few extra pieces.

III. Make Single Triangles. The inner Full/Queen Quilt requires 192 single triangles (96 of each fabric) for the Ocean Waves units. No single triangles are needed in the border.

To make single triangles, cut 48 3⅜" squares from each fabric. Cut each square in half diagonally to make two single triangles.

IV. Construct Ocean Waves Quilt Units. Refer to the Unit Chart and combine quick-pieced triangle-squares, single triangles and setting pieces to make the units needed.

V. Set the Quilt Top. Sew A-d units together in seven vertical rows as shown in Figure 1. Sew the rows together to form the quilt top.

VI. Add the Borders. Referring to Figure 1, combine 256 triangle-squares to form zig-zag borders. The two side borders use 68 triangle-squares each, the top and bottom borders, 60 each. Add fabric and pieced borders to quilt top. See the General Instructions for tips on adding and mitering border seams.

Note: The zig-zag border can be made as shown in Figure 1, a dark zig-zag on a light background, or as shown in Figure 2, a light zig-zag on a dark background. The same number of triangle-squares (256) is required for either version.

Figure 1, Full/Queen Quilt.

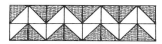

Figure 2

Twin Coverlet 60" x 80"

I. Cut Borders and Setting Pieces.
From Fabric #1, cut: 2 outer borders, 3" x 83"
2 inner borders, 3" x 68"
2 outer borders, 3" x 63"
2 inner borders, 3" x 48"

From Fabric #2, cut: setting pieces, 8 A squares
6 BC triangles
4 D triangles

II. Make Quick-Pieced Triangle-Squares. From remaining Fabric #1 and Fabric #2, cut or tear seven 18" x 22" pieces of each fabric.

Combine the fabric pieces to make 2½″ finished triangle-squares. Use Grid #9 for your marking pattern, marking a grid of 3⅜″ squares. This grid arrangement makes 60 triangle-squares per combination, a total of 420 triangle-squares, once all seven combinations are sewn.

The Twin Coverlet requires a total of 432 triangle squares (240 of them for the inner quilt and 192 for the zig-zag border), so you need 12 more triangle-squares. To make the additional triangle-squares, you will need a 9″ x 19″ x piece of each fabric. Pair, mark and sew, using Grid #4 for your marking pattern. This grid arrangement produces 20 triangle-squares, which will provide a few extra pieces.

III. Make Single Triangles. The inner Twin Coverlet requires 96 single triangles (48 of each fabric) for the Ocean Waves units. No single triangles are needed in the border.

To make single triangles, cut 24 3⅜″ squares from each fabric. Cut each square in half diagonally to make two single triangles.

IV. Construct Ocean Waves Quilt Units. Refer to the Unit Chart and combine quick-pieced triangle-squares, single triangles and setting pieces to make the A, a, B, C, D and d units needed.

V. Set the Quilt Top. Sew A-d units together in five vertical rows as shown in Figure 3. Join the rows to form the quilt top.

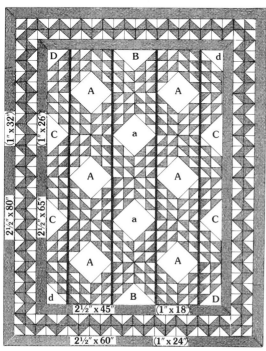

Figure 3, Twin Coverlet. (Measurements in parentheses are for Doll Quilt.)

VI. Add the Borders. Referring to Figure 3, combine 192 triangle-squares to form zig-zag borders. The two side borders use 52 triangle-squares each, the top and bottom borders, 44 each. Add fabric and pieced borders to quilt top.

Note: The zig-zag border can be made as shown in Figure 3, a dark zig-zag on a light background, or as shown in Figure 2, a light zig-zag on a dark background. The same number of triangle-squares (192) is required for either version.

Doll Quilt 24″ x 32″

I. Cut Borders and Setting Pieces.
From Fabric #1, cut: 2 outer borders, 1½″ x 35″
2 inner borders, 1½″ x 29″
2 outer borders, 1½″ x 27″
2 inner borders, 1½″ x 21″

From Fabric #, cut: setting pieces, 8 A squares
6 BC triangles
4 D triangles

II. Make Quick-Pieced Triangle-Squares. From remaining Fabric #1 and Fabric #2, cut or tear two 18″ x 22″ pieces of each fabric.

Combine the fabric pieces to make one-inch finished triangle-squares. Use Grid #13 for your marking pattern, marking a grid of 1⅞″ squares.

This grid arrangement makes 198 triangle-squares per combination, a total of 396 triangle-squares, once both combinations are sewn.

The Doll Quilt requires a total of 432 triangle squares (240 of them for the inner quilt and 192 for the zig-zag border), so you need 36 more triangle-squares. To make the additional triangle-squares, you will need a 5″ x 19″ piece of each fabric. Pair, mark and sew, using Grid #7 as your marking pattern. This grid arrangement produces the needed extra pieces.

III. Make Single Triangles. The inner Doll Quilt requires 96 single triangles (48 of each fabric) for the Ocean Waves units. No single triangles are needed in the border.

To make single triangles, cut 24 1⅞″ squares from each fabric. Cut each square in half diagonally to make two single triangles.

IV. Follow instructions IV through VI for Twin Coverlet to complete Doll Quilt.

Wall Quilt 60″ x 60″

I. Cut Borders and Setting Pieces.
From Fabric #1, cut: 4 outer borders, 3″ x 63″
4 inner borders, 3″ x 48″

From Fabric #2, cut: setting pieces, 5 A squares
4 BC triangles
4 D triangles

II. Make Quick-Pieced Triangle-Squares.
From remaining Fabric #1 and Fabric #2, cut or tear five 18″ x 22″ pieces of each fabric.

Combine the fabric pieces to make 2½″ finished triangle-squares. Use Grid #9 for your marking pattern, marking a grid of 3⅜″ squares.

This grid arrangement makes 60 triangle-squares per combination, a total of 300 triangle-squares, once all five combinations are sewn.

The Wall Quilt requires a total of 320 triangle squares (160 of them for the inner quilt and 160 for the zig-zag border), so you need 20 more triangle-squares. To make the additional triangle-squares, you will need a 9″ x 19″ piece of each fabric. Pair, mark and sew, using Grid #4 as your marking pattern. This grid arrangement produces the needed extra pieces.

III. Make Single Triangles.
The inner Wall Quilt requires 64 single triangles (32 of each fabric) for the Ocean Waves units. No single triangles are needed in the border.

To make single triangles, cut 16 3⅜″ squares of each fabric. Cut each square in half diagonally to make two single triangles.

IV. Construct Ocean Waves Quilt Units.
Refer to the Unit Chart and combine quick-pieced triangle-squares, single triangles and setting pieces to make the A, a, B, C, D and d units needed.

V. Set the Quilt Top.
Sew A-d units together in five vertical rows as shown in Figure 4. Sew the rows together to form the quilt top.

VI. Add the Borders.
Referring to Figure 4, combine 160 triangle-squares to form zig-zag borders. The two side borders use 36 triangle-squares each, the top and bottom borders, 44 each. Add fabric and pieced borders to quilt top.

Note: The zig-zag border can be made as shown in Figure 4, a dark zig-zag on a light background, or as shown in Figure 2, a light zig-zag on a dark background. The same number of triangle-squares (160) is required for either version.

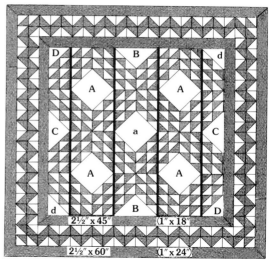

Figure 4, Wall Quilt. (Measurements in parentheses are for Mini Wall Quilt.)

Mini Wall Quilt 24″ x 24″

I. Cut Borders and Setting Pieces.
From Fabric #1, cut: 4 outer borders, 1½″ x 27″
4 inner borders, 1½″ x 21″

From Fabric #2, cut: setting pieces, 5 A squares
4 BC triangles
4 D triangles

II. Make Quick-Pieced Triangle-Squares.
From remaining Fabric #1 and Fabric #2, cut or tear an 18″ x 22″ piece of each fabric.

Combine the fabric pieces to make one-inch finished triangle-squares. Use Grid #13 for your marking pattern, marking a grid of 1⅞″ squares.

This grid arrangement makes 198 triangle-squares. The Mini Wall Quilt requires a total of 320 triangle squares (160 of them for the inner quilt and 160 for the zig-zag border), so you need 122 more triangle-squares. To make the additional triangle-squares, you will need a 13″ x 22″ piece of each fabric. Pair, mark and sew, using Grid #11. This grid arrangement produces 132 triangle-squares, so you will have a few extra pieces.

III. Make Single Triangles.
The inner Mini Wall Quilt requires 64 single triangles (32 of each fabric) for the Ocean Waves units. No single triangles are needed in the border.

To make single triangles, cut 16 1⅞″ squares of each fabric. Cut each square in half diagonally to make two single triangles.

IV.
Follow instructions IV through VI for Wall Quilt to complete Mini Wall Quilt.

Contrast-Set Ocean Waves

The Contrast-Set Ocean Waves Quilt calls for just two fabrics used over and over to make the triangles, and a third fabric used only for the setting pieces. The Mini Wall Quilt in Photo 22 is made of three dark Amish solids. For the Doll Quilt in Photo 21, blue and white triangles were set with red.

Borders and Setting Pieces

The quilts in this book in this variation have zig-zag middle borders. The cutting measurements for the fabric borders include ¼" seam allowances. Borders are first cut a few inches longer than needed. The borders will be trimmed to exact length when added to the quilt top. Refer to pages 18–19 for instructions on marking and cutting the setting pieces.

Yardages for Contrast-Set Ocean Waves

Yardages are for 44"–45" wide fabric.

Full/Queen Quilt 80" x 100"

3¼ yards Fabric #1 for triangles

4½ yards Fabric #2 for triangles and borders

3¼ yards Fabric #3 (contrast) for setting pieces and border triangles

¾ yard fabric for binding   6 yards for backing

Twin Coverlet 60" x 80"

2½ yards Fabric #1 for triangles

3½ yards Fabric #2 for triangles and borders

2¼ yards Fabric #3 (contrast) for setting pieces and border triangles

¾ yard fabric for binding   5 yards for backing

Doll Quilt 24" x 32"

1¼ yards Fabric #1 for triangles

1¼ yards Fabric #2 for triangles and borders

¾ yard Fabric #3 (contrast) for setting pieces and border triangles

¼ yard fabric for binding   1 yard for backing

Wall Quilt 60" x 60"

2 yards Fabric #1 for triangles

2½ yards Fabric #2 for triangles and borders

1¾ yards Fabric #3 (contrast) for setting pieces and border triangles

½ yard fabric for binding   3½ yards for backing

Mini Wall Quilt 24" x 24"

1 yard Fabric #1 for triangles

1 yard Fabric #2 for triangles and borders

¾ yard Fabric #3 (contrast) for setting pieces and border triangles

¼ yard fabric for binding   1 yard for backing

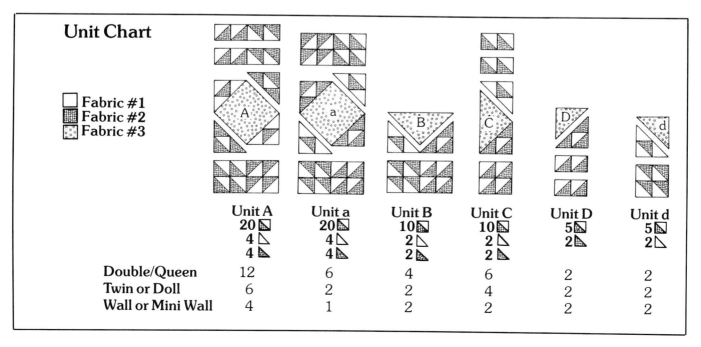

	Unit A	Unit a	Unit B	Unit C	Unit D	Unit d
	20	20	10	10	5	5
	4	4	2	2	2	2
	4	4	2	2		
Double/Queen	12	6	4	6	2	2
Twin or Doll	6	2	2	4	2	2
Wall or Mini Wall	4	1	2	2	2	2

Fabric #1
Fabric #2
Fabric #3

Full/Queen Quilt 80" x 100"

I. Cut Borders and Setting Pieces.

From Fabric #2, cut: 2 outer borders, 3" x 103"
                       2 inner borders, 3" x 88"
                       2 outer borders, 3" x 83"
                       2 inner borders, 3" x 68"

From Fabric #3
(contrast) cut: setting pieces, 18 A squares
                       10 BC triangles
                       4 D triangles

II. Make Quick-Pieced Triangle-Squares.

The Contrast-Set Ocean Waves quilt requires two different kinds of triangle-squares, those that are a combination of Fabrics #1 and #2, (used in the inner quilt top) and those that are a combinations of Fabrics #1 and #3 (used in the zig-zag border).

Fabric #1 and #2 combination:

From Fabrics #1 and #2, cut or tear eight 18" x 22" pieces of each fabric. Refer to the General Instructions section of this book and combine the fabric pieces to make 2½" finished triangle-squares. Use Grid #9 for your marking pattern, marking a grid of 3⅜" squares.

The Grid #9 arrangement makes 60 triangle-squares per combination, a total of 480 triangle-squares once all eight combinations are sewn. This is the exact number of triangle-squares needed for the inner quilt top of the Full/Queen Quilt.

Fabric #1 and #3 combination:

From Fabrics #1 and #3, cut or tear four 18" x 22" pieces of each fabric. Combine these fabrics in the same manner as for Fabrics #1 and #2 to make 2½" finished triangle-squares. The four combinations will produce 240 triangle-squares. The zig-zag border for the Full/Queen Quilt requires 256 triangle-squares, so you need 16 more triangle-squares. To make the additional triangle-squares, you will need a 9" x 19" piece of each fabric. Pair, mark and sew, using Grid #4. The Grid #4 arrangement produces 20 triangle-squares, which will provide a few extra pieces.

III. Make Single Triangles.

The inner Full/Queen Quilt requires 192 single triangles (96 each of Fabrics #1 and #2) for the Ocean Waves units. No single triangles are needed in the border.

To make single triangles, cut 48 3⅜" squares from each fabric. Cut each square in half diagonally to make two single triangles.

IV. Construct Ocean Waves Quilt Units.

Refer to the Unit Chart and combine quick-pieced triangle-squares, single triangles and setting pices to make the A, a, B, C, D and d units needed for the Full/Queen quilt. See the Box on page 20 for tips on sewing and pressing units.

V. Set the Quilt Top.

Sew A-d units together in seven vertical rows as shown in Figure 1. Join the rows to form the quilt top.

VI. Add the Borders.

Referring to Figure 1, combine the Fabric #1 and #3 triangle-squares to form the zig-zag border. The two side borders use 68 triangle-squares each, the top and bottom borders, 60 each. Add fabric and pieced borders to quilt top. See General Instructions for tips on adding and mitering borders.

Note that the zig-zag border can be made as shown in Figure 1, with the contrast fabric forming the zig-zag, or as shown in Figure 2, with the contrast fabric forming the background of the border. The same number of triangle-squares (256) is required for either version.

Figure 1, Full/Queen Quilt.

Figure 2

Twin Coverlet 60" x 80"

I. Cut Borders and Setting Pieces.
From Fabric #2, cut: 2 outer borders, 3" x 83"
                                   2 inner borders, 3" x 68"
                                   2 outer borders, 3" x 63"
                                   2 inner borders, 3" x 48"

From Fabric #3
(contrast), cut: setting pieces, 8 A squares
                                   6 BC triangles
                                   4 D triangles

II. Make Quick-Pieced Triangle-Squares.
The Contrast-Set Ocean Waves quilt requires two different kinds of triangle-squares, those that are a combination of Fabric #1 and #2, (used in the inner quilt top) and those that are a combinations of Fabric #1 and #3 (used in the zig-zag border).

Fabric #1 and #2 combination:
From Fabrics #1 and #2, cut or tear four 18" x 22" pieces of each fabric.

Combine the fabric pieces to make 2½" finished triangle-squares. Use Grid #9 for your marking pattern, marking a grid of 3⅜" squares.

The Grid #9 arrangement makes 60 triangle-squares per combination, a total of 240 triangle-squares once all four combinations are sewn. This is the exact number of triangle-squares needed for the inner quilt top of the Twin Coverlet.

Fabric #1 and #3 combination:
From Fabrics #1 and #3, cut or tear three 18" x 22" pieces of each fabric. Combine these fabrics in the same manner as for Fabrics #1 and #2 to make 2½" finished triangle-squares. The three combinations will produce 180 triangle-squares. The zig-zag border for the Twin Coverlet requires 192 triangle-squares, so you need 12 more. To make the additional triangle-squares, you will need a 9" x 19" piece of each fabric. Pair, mark and sew, using Grid #4. The Grid #4 arrangement produces 20 triangle-squares, which will provide a few extra pieces.

III. Make Single Triangles.
The inner Twin Coverlet requires 96 single triangles (48 each of Fabrics #1 and #2) for the Ocean Waves units. No single triangles are needed in the border.

To make single triangles, cut 24 3⅜" squares from each fabric. Cut each square in half diagonally to make two single triangles.

IV. Construct Ocean Waves Quilt Units.
Refer to the Unit Chart and combine quick-pieced triangle-squares, single triangles and setting pieces to make the A, a, B, C, D and d units needed.

V. Set the Quilt Top.
Sew A-d units together in five vertical rows as shown in Figure 3. Join the rows to form the quilt top.

VI. Add the Borders.
Referring to Figure 3, combine 192 Fabric #1 and #3 triangle-squares to form zig-zag borders. The two side borders use 52 triangle-squares each, the top and bottom borders, 44 each. Add fabric and pieced borders to quilt top.

Note that the zig-zag border can be made as shown in Figure 3, a contrast zig-zag on a light background, or as shown in Figure 2, a light zig-zag on a contrast background. The same number of triangle-squares (192) is required for either version.

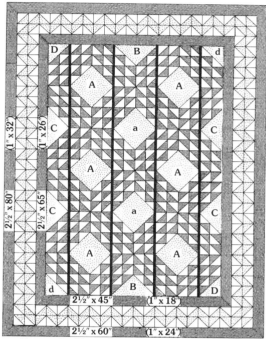

Figure 3, Twin Coverlet. (Measurements in parentheses are for Doll Quilt.)

Doll Quilt 24" x 24"

I. Cut Borders and Setting Pieces.
From Fabric #2, cut: 2 outer borders, 1½" x 35"
                                   2 inner borders, 1½" x 29"
                                   2 outer borders, 1½" x 27"
                                   2 inner borders, 1½" x 21"

From Fabric #3
(contrast), cut: setting pieces, 8 A squares
                                   6 BC triangles
                                   4 D triangles

II. Make Quick-Pieced Triangle-Squares.
The Contrast-Set Ocean Waves quilt requires two different kinds of triangle-squares, those that are a combination of Fabric #1 and #2, (used in the inner quilt top) and those that are a combination of Fabric #1 and #3 (used in the zig-zag border).

Fabric #1 and #2 combination:
From Fabrics #1 and #2, cut or tear an 18" x 22" piece of each fabric.

Combine the fabric pieces to make one-inch finished triangle-squares. Use Grid #13 for your marking pattern, marking a grid of 1⅞" squares.

The Grid #13 arrangement makes 198 triangle-squares. The inner Doll Quilt requires 240 triangle-squares, so you need 42 more triangle-squares. To make the additional triangle-squares, you will need a 10" x 14" piece of Fabrics #1 and #2. Pair, mark and sew, using Grid #8. The Grid #8 arrangement produces 48 triangle-squares, so you will have a few pieces left over.

Fabric #1 and #3 combination:
From Fabrics #1 and #3, cut or tear one 18" x 22" piece of each fabric. Combine these fabrics in the same manner as for Fabrics #1 and #2 to make one-inch finished triangle-squares. Use Grid #13. The combination will produce 198 triangle-squares. The zig-zag border for the Doll Quilt requires 192 triangle-squares, so you will have a few pieces left over.

III. Make Single Triangles. The inner Doll Quilt requires 96 single triangles (48 each of Fabrics #1 and #2) for the Ocean Waves units. No single triangles are needed in the border.
To make single triangles, cut 24 1⅞" squares from each fabric. Cut each square in half diagonally to make two single triangles.

IV. Follow instructions IV through VI for Twin Coverlet to complete Doll Quilt.

Wall Quilt 60" x 60"

I. Cut Borders and Setting Pieces.
From Fabric #2, cut: 4 outer borders, 3" x 63"
                      4 inner borders, 3" x 48"

From Fabric #3
(contrast), cut: setting pieces, 5 A squares
                  4 BC triangles
                  4 D triangles

II. Make Quick-Pieced Triangle-Squares. The Contrast-Set Ocean Waves quilt requires two different kinds of triangle-squares, those that are a combination of Fabrics #1 and #2, (used in the inner quilt top) and those that are a combinations of Fabrics #1 and #3 (used in the zig-zag border).

Fabric #1 and #2 combination:
From Fabrics #1 and #2, cut or tear three 18" x 22" pieces of each fabric. Combine the fabric pieces to make 2½" finished triangle-squares. Use Grid #9 for your marking pattern, marking a grid of 3⅜" squares.
The Grid #9 arrangement makes 60 triangle-squares per combination, a total of 180 triangle-squares once all three combinations are sewn. The

inner Wall Quilt requires 160 triangle-squares, so you will have a few extra pieces.

Fabric #1 and #3 combination:
From Fabrics #1 and #3, cut or tear three 18" x 22" pieces of each fabric. Combine these fabrics in the same manner as for Fabrics #1 and #2 to make 2½" finished triangle-squares. Use Grid #9. The four combinations will produce 180 triangle-squares. The zig-zag border for the Wall Quilt requires 160 triangle-squares, so you will have a few pieces left over.

III. Make Single Triangles. The inner Wall Quilt requires 64 single triangles (32 each of Fabrics #1 and #2) for the Ocean Waves units. No single triangles are needed in the border.
To make single triangles, cut 16 3⅜" squares from each fabric. Cut each square in half diagonally to make two single triangles.

IV. Construct Ocean Waves Quilt Units. Refer to the Unit Chart and combine quick-pieced triangle squares, single triangles and setting pieces to make the needed, A, a, B, C, D and d units for your quilt.

V. Set the Quilt Top. Sew A-d units together in five vertical rows as shown in Figure 4. Sew the rows together to form the quilt top.

VI. Add the Borders. Referring to Figure 4, combine 160 Fabric #1 and #3 triangle-squares to form zig-zag borders. The two side borders use 36 triangle-squares each, the top and bottom borders, 44 each. Add fabric and pieced borders to quilt top.
Note that the zig-zag border can be made as shown in Figure 4, a dark zig-zag on a light background, or as shown in Figure 2, a light zig-zag on a dark background. The same number of triangle-squares (160) is required for either version.

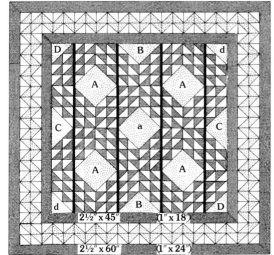

Figure 4, Wall Quilt. (Measurements in parentheses are for Mini Wall Quilt.)

21 Bright red setting squares and triangles, and a red zig-zag border, give this Contrast-Set Doll Quilt a crisp, cheerful character. (Contrast-Set Ocean Waves, 24" x 32", 1988, Liz Porter.)

22 This Amish-style Mini Wall Quilt uses slate blue and plum for the triangle-squares, with a darker solid blue for the contrasting setting pieces. Iowan Dorothy Crowdes pieced and hand quilted it. (Contrast-Set Ocean Waves, 24" x 24", 1988, Dorothy Crowdes.)

Mini Wall Quilt 24" x 24"

I. Cut Borders and Setting Pieces.
From Fabric #2, cut: 4 outer borders, 1½" x 27"
4 inner borders, 1½" x 21"

From Fabric #3
(contrast), cut: setting pieces, 5 A squares
4 BC triangles
4 D triangles

II. Make Quick-Pieced Triangle-Squares. The Contrast-Set Ocean Waves quilt requires two different kinds of triangle-squares, those that are a combination of Fabrics #1 and #2, (used in the inner quilt top) and those that are a combination of Fabrics #1 and #3 (used in the zig-zag border).

Fabric #1 and #2 combination:
From Fabrics #1 and #2, cut or tear one 18" x 22" piece of each fabric. Combine the fabric pieces to make one-inch finished triangle-squares. Use Grid #13 for your marking pattern, marking a grid of 1⅞" squares.

The Grid #13 arrangement makes 198 triangle-squares. The inner Mini Wall Quilt requires 160 triangle-squares, so you will have a few pieces left over.

Fabric #1 and #3 combination:
From Fabrics #1 and #3, cut or tear one 18" x 22" piece of each fabric. Combine these fabrics in the same manner as for Fabrics #1 and #2, using Grid #13, to make one-inch finished triangle-squares. The combination will produce 198 triangle-squares. The zig-zag border for the Wall Quilt requires 160 triangle-squares, so you will have a few pieces left over.

III. Make Single Triangles. The inner Wall Quilt requires 64 single triangles (32 each of Fabrics #1 and #2) for the Ocean Waves units. No single triangles are needed in the border.

To make single triangles, cut 16 1⅞" squares from each fabric. Cut each square in half diagonally to make two single triangles.

IV. Follow instructions IV through VI for Wall Quilt to complete Mini Wall Quilt.

Pinwheel Ocean Waves

For the Pinwheel Ocean Waves variation, most of the triangle-squares in the quilt are made of the same two fabrics but a contrasting third fabric is introduced to make triangle-squares for the pinwheels. The Wall Quilt example in Photo 24 combines a country-style red and green plaid with a natural print for the majority of the triangles, with a dark green print for the pinwheels. Beautiful blue floral prints were combined for the Full/Queen example in photo 23. The Doll Quilt in Photo 25 uses shades of peach and green, with a muted rust for the pinwheels.

Borders and Setting Pieces

All the Pinwheel Ocean Waves quilts in this book have three fabric borders with extra pinwheels set in the corners of the middle border. The cutting measurements for fabric borders include ¼" seam allowances. Borders are first cut a few inches longer than needed. Borders will be trimmed to exact length when added to the quilt top. Refer to pages 18–19 for instructions on marking and cutting the setting pieces.

Yardages for Pinwheel Ocean Waves

Yardages are for 44"–45" wide fabric.

Full/Queen Quilt 80" x 100"

6 yards Fabric #1 for triangles, pinwheel triangles, middle borders and setting pieces

5 yards Fabric #2 for triangles and borders

¾ yard Fabric #3 (contrast) for triangles

¾ yard Fabric for binding   6 yards for backing

Twin Coverlet 60" x 80"

4 yards Fabric #1 for triangles, pinwheel triangles, middle borders and setting pieces

3 yards Fabric #2 for triangles and borders

¾ yard Fabric #3 (contrast) for pinwheel triangles

¾ yard fabric for binding   5 yards for backing

Doll Quilt 24" x 32"

1½ yards Fabric #1 for triangles, pinwheel triangles, middle borders and setting pieces

1¼ yards Fabric #2 for triangles and borders

½ yard Fabric #3 (contrast) for pinwheel triangles

¼ yard fabric for binding   1 yard for backing

Wall Quilt 50" x 50"

2 yards Fabric #1 for triangles, pinwheel triangles, middle borders and setting pieces

1½ yards Fabric #2 for triangles and borders

½ yard Fabric #3 (contrast) for pinwheel triangles

½ yard fabric for binding   3½ yards for backing

Mini Wall Quilt 20" x 20"

¾ yard Fabric #1 for triangles, pinwheel triangles and setting pieces

1 yard Fabric #2 for triangles and borders

¼ yard Fabric #3 (contrast) for pinwheel triangles

¼ yard fabric for binding   1 yard for backing

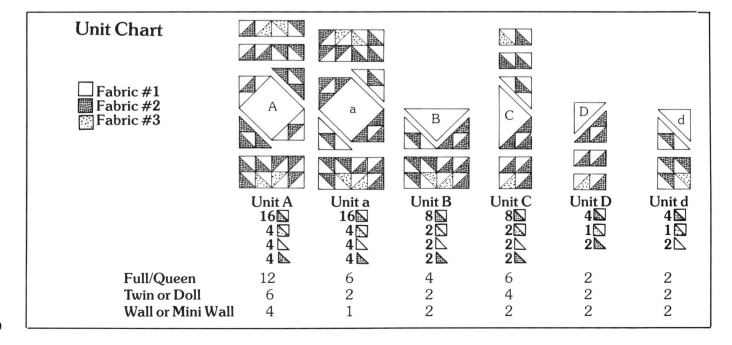

Unit Chart		Unit A	Unit a	Unit B	Unit C	Unit D	Unit d
☐ Fabric #1		16	16	8	8	4	4
▦ Fabric #2		4	4	2	2	1	1
▨ Fabric #3		4	4	2	2	2	2
		4	4	2	2		
Full/Queen		12	6	4	6	2	2
Twin or Doll		6	2	2	4	2	2
Wall or Mini Wall		4	1	2	2	2	2

Full/Queen Quilt 80″ x 100″

I. Cut Borders and Setting Pieces.
From Fabric #1, cut: 2 middle borders, 5½″ x 88″
2 middle borders, 5½″ x 68″
setting pieces, 18 A squares
10 BC triangles
4 D triangles

From Fabric #2, cut: 2 outer borders, 3″ x 103″
2 inner borders, 3″ x 88″
2 outer borders, 3″ x 83″
2 inner borders, 3″ x 68″

II. Make Quick-Pieced Triangle-Squares.
The Pinwheel Ocean Waves Quilt requires two different kinds of triangle-squares, those that are a combination of Fabrics #1 and #2 and those that are a combination of Fabrics #1 and #3 (for the pinwheels).

Fabric #1 and #2 combination:
From Fabrics #1 and #2, cut or tear six 18″ x 22″ pieces of each fabric. Refer to the General Instructions section of this book and combine the fabric pieces to make 2½″ finished triangle-squares. Use Grid #9 for your marking pattern, marking a grid of 3⅜″ squares.

The Grid #9 arrangement makes 60 triangle-squares per combination, a total of 360 triangle-squares once all six combinations are sewn. The Full/Queen Quilt requires 384 Fabric #1/#2 triangle-squares, so you need 24 more. To make the additional triangle-squares, you will need a 9″ x 22″ piece of each fabric. Pair, mark and sew, using Grid #5. This grid arrangement produces the additional triangle-squares.

Fabric #1 and #3 combination:
From Fabrics #1 and #3, cut or tear two 18″ x 22″ pieces of each fabric. Combine these fabrics in the same manner as for Fabrics #1 and #2 to make 2½″ finished triangle-squares. Use Grid #9. The two combinations will produce 120 triangle-squares. The Full/Queen Quilt requires 112 Fabric #1/#3 triangle-squares, so you will have a few pieces left over.

III. Make Single Triangles.
The inner Full/Queen Quilt requires 192 single triangles (96 each of Fabrics #1 and #2) for the Ocean Waves units. To make the single triangles, cut 48 3⅜″ squares from each fabric. Cut each square in half diagonally to make two single triangles.

IV. Construct Ocean Waves Quilt Units.
Refer to the Unit Chart and combine quick-pieced triangle-squares, single triangles and setting pieces to make the needed A-d units for the Full/Queen Quilt. See the Box on page 20 for the tips on sewing and pressing units.

V. Set the Quilt Top.
Sew A-d units together in seven vertical rows as shown in Figure 1. Join the rows to form the quilt top.

VI. Add the Borders.
Sew the inner Fabric #2 borders to the four sides of the quilt top. See General Instructions for tips on mitering border seams.

Combine four of the Fabric #1/#3 triangle-squares to make a pinwheel. Make a total of four pinwheels.

Sew the Fabric #1 border strips to the sides of the quilt top. Sew pinwheels to the ends of the top and bottom Fabric #1 border strips. Sew top and bottom borders to the quilt top.

Sew the outer Fabric #2 borders to quilt top. Miter seams.

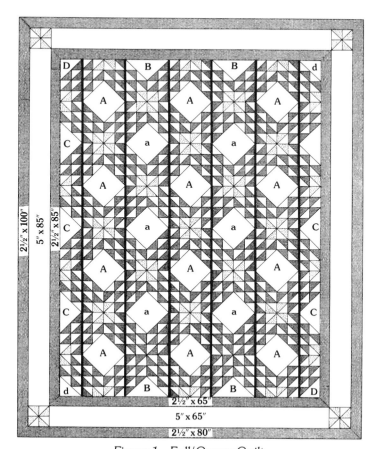

Figure 1, Full/Queen Quilt.

23   Two flowery blue-gray prints were combined for the triangle-squares in this Full/Queen Pinwheel Ocean Waves. The darker blue pinwheel blocks between the Ocean Waves units contrast well in this quilt by Iowans Ilene Kagarice and Martha Street, who have been sewing companions for many years. When a team project is at the quilting stage, Martha works diligently at it through the day and then turns it over to Ilene who stops by Martha's farm on the way home from work. (Pinwheel Ocean Waves, 80″ x 100″, 1988, Ilene Kagarice and Martha Street.)

Wall Quilt 50″ x 50″

1½ yards Fabric #1 for triangles

2¾ yards Fabric #2 for triangles, setting triangles and border

½ yard fabric for binding   3½ yards for backing

Mini Wall Quilt 20″ x 20″

¾ yard Fabric #1 for triangles and setting triangles

1 yard Fabric #2 for triangles, setting triangles and border

¼ yard fabric for binding   1 yard for backing

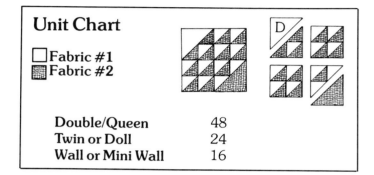

Unit Chart		
□ Fabric #1		
▨ Fabric #2		
Double/Queen	48	
Twin or Doll	24	
Wall or Mini Wall	16	

Full/Queen Quilt 80″ x 100″

I. Cut Borders and Strips for Setting Triangles.

From Fabric #1, cut: 2 middle borders, 5½″ x 98″
2 middle borders, 5½″ x 78″
4 strips, 5⅞″ x 44″, for D setting triangles

From Fabric #2, cut: 2 outer borders, 3″ x 103″
2 inner borders, 3″ x 88″
2 outer borders, 3″ x 83″
2 inner borders, 3″ x 68″
4 strips, 5⅞″ x 44″, for D setting triangles

II. Make Quick-Pieced Triangle-Squares.
From Fabrics #1 and #2, cut or tear eight 18″ x 22″ pieces of each fabric. Refer to the General Instructions section of this book (pages 11–22) and combine the fabric pieces to make 2½″ finished triangle-squares. Use Grid #9 for your marking pattern, marking a grid of 3⅜″ squares.

The Grid #9 arrangement makes 60 triangle-squares per combination, a total of 480 triangle-squares once all eight combinations are sewn. This is the exact number of triangle-squares needed for the Full/Queen Quilt.

III. Make Single Triangles.
The Full/Queen Quilt requires 192 single triangles (96 of each fabric) for the Ocean Wave units. To make the single triangles, cut 48 3⅜″ squares from each fabric. Cut each square in half diagonally to make two single triangles.

IV. Cut Setting Pieces.
Cut the 5⅞″ strips of Fabric #1 and Fabric #2 into 24 squares, each 5⅞″ square, from each fabric. Cut the squares in half diagonally to make 48 D setting triangles of each fabric.

V. Construct Ocean Waves Quilt Units.
Refer to the Unit Chart and combine quick-pieced triangle-squares and D setting triangles to form the required number of units for the Full/Queen quilt.

VI. Set the Quilt Top.
Refer to Figure 1 and join units in six vertical rows of eight units per row, rotating the units to create the split centers.

VII. Add the Borders.
Center and sew the inner, middle and outer borders together to make two sets of three long side borders and two sets of three shorter borders.

Treating each border set as a single unit, center and stitch a border set to each side of the quilt top. Stitch the long borders to the sides of the quilt top and the short borders to the top and bottom.

Miter the border corner seams.

Figure 1, Full/Queen Quilt.

Twin Coverlet 60″ x 80″

I. Cut Borders and Strips For Setting Triangles.
From Fabric #1, cut: 2 middle borders, 5½″ x 78″
2 middle borders, 5½″ x 58″
2 strips, 5⅞″ x 44″, for D
    setting triangles

From Fabric #2, cut: 2 outer borders, 3″ x 83″
2 inner borders, 3″ x 68″
2 outer borders, 3″ x 63″
2 inner borders, 3″ x 48″
2 strips, 5⅞″ x 44″, for D
    setting triangles

II. Make Quick-Pieced Triangle-Squares. From Fabrics #1 and #2, cut or tear four 18″ x 22″ pieces of each fabric. Combine the fabric pieces to make 2½″ finished triangle-squares. Use Grid #9 for your marking pattern, marking a grid of 3⅜″ squares.

The Grid #9 arrangement makes 60 triangle-squares per combination, a total of 240 triangle-squares once all four combinations are sewn. This is the exact number of triangle-squares needed for the Twin Coverlet.

III. Make Single Triangles. The Twin Coverlet requires 96 single triangles (48 of each fabric) for the Ocean Waves units. To make the single triangles, cut 24 squares, each 3⅜″ square, from each fabric. Cut each square in half diagonally to make two single triangles.

IV. Cut Setting Pieces. Cut the 5⅞″ strips of Fabric #1 and Fabric #2 into 12 squares, each 5⅞″ square, of each fabric. Cut the squares in half diagonally to make 24 D setting triangles of each fabric.

V. Construct Ocean Waves Quilt Units. Refer to the Unit Chart and combine quick-pieced triangle-squares and D setting triangles to form the required number of units for your quilt.

VI. Set the Quilt Top. Refer to Figure 2 and join units in four vertical rows of six units per row, rotating the units to create the split centers.

VII. Follow Instruction VII for Full/Queen Quilt to complete Twin Coverlet.

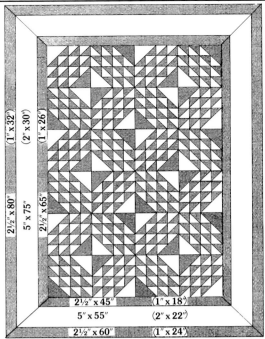

Figure 2, Twin Coverlet. (Measurements in parentheses are for Doll Quilt.)

Doll Quilt 24″ x 32″

I. Cut Borders and Strips for Setting Triangles.
From Fabric #1, cut: 2 middle borders, 2½″ x 33″
2 middle borders, 2½″ x 25″
1 strip, 2⅞″ x 44″, for D
    setting triangles

From Fabric #2, cut: 2 outer borders, 1½″ x 35″
2 inner borders, 1½″ x 29″
2 outer borders, 1½″ x 27″
2 inner borders, 1½″ x 21″
1 strip, 2⅞″ x 44″, for D
    setting triangles

II. Make Quick-Pieced Triangle-Squares. From Fabrics #1 and #2, cut or tear one 18″ x 22″ piece of each fabric. Combine the fabric pieces to make one-inch finished triangle-squares. Use Grid #13 for your marking pattern, marking a grid of 1⅞″ squares.

The Grid #13 arrangement makes 198 triangle-squares. The Doll Quilt requires 240 triangle-squares, so you need 42 more.

To make the additional triangle-squares, you will need a 10″ x 14″ piece of each fabric. Pair, mark and sew, using Grid #8 for your marking pattern. This grid arrangement produces 48 triangle-squares, so you will have a few pieces left over.

III. Make Single Triangles. The Doll Quilt requires 96 single triangles (48 of each fabric) for the Ocean Waves units. To make the single triangles, cut 24 1⅞″ squares from each fabric. Cut each square in half diagonally to make two single triangles.

IV. Cut Setting Pieces. Cut the 2⅞" strips of Fabric #1 and Fabric #2 into 12 squares, each 2⅞" square, of each fabric. Cut the squares in half diagonally to make 24 D setting triangles of each fabric.

V. Follow instructions V through VII for Twin Coverlet above to complete Doll Quilt.

Wall Quilt 50" x 50"

I. Cut Borders and Strips for Setting Triangles.
From Fabric #1, cut: 1 strip, 5⅞" x 44", for D setting triangles
1 square, 5⅞" x 5⅞" for extra D setting triangles

From Fabric #2, cut: 4 borders, 5½" x 53"
1 strip, 5⅞" x 44", for D setting triangles
1 square, 5⅞" x 5⅞" for extra D triangles

II. Make Quick-Pieced Triangle-Squares. From Fabrics #1 and #2, cut or tear three 18" x 22" pieces of each fabric. Combine the fabric pieces to make 2½" finished triangle-squares. Use Grid #9 for your marking pattern, marking a grid of 3⅜" squares.

The Grid #9 arrangement makes 60 triangle-squares per combination, a total of 180 triangle-squares once all three combinations are sewn. The Wall Quilt requires 160 triangle-squares, so you will have a few pieces left over.

III. Make Single Triangles. The Wall Quilt requires 64 single triangles (32 of each fabric) for the Ocean Waves units. To make the single triangles, cut 16 3⅜" squares from each fabric. Cut each square in half diagonally to make two single triangles.

IV. Cut Setting Pieces. Cut the 5⅞" strips of Fabric #1 and Fabric #2 into seven 5⅞" squares of each fabric. Cut the squares in half diagonally to make 14 D setting triangles of each fabric. Cut the extra 5⅞" square in half diagonally. You will have 16 D triangles of each fabric.

V. Construct Ocean Waves Quilt Units. Refer to the Unit Chart and combine quick-pieced triangle-squares and D setting triangles to form the required number of units for your quilt.

VI. Set the Quilt Top. Refer to Figure 3 and join units in four vertical rows of four units per row, rotating the units to create the split centers.

VII. Add the Borders. Center and sew borders to the quilt top, mitering corners.

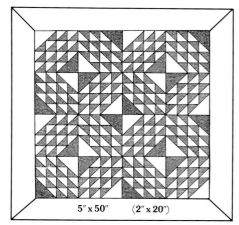

5" x 50"   (2" x 20")

Figure 3, Wall Quilt. (Measurements in parentheses are for Mini Wall Quilt.)

Mini Wall Quilt 20" x 20"

I. Cut Borders and Strips for Setting Triangles.
From Fabric #1, cut: 1 strip, 2⅞" x 44", for D setting triangles

From Fabric #2, cut: 4 borders, 2½" x 23"
1 strip, 2⅞" x 44", for D setting triangles

II. Make Quick-Pieced Triangle-Squares. From Fabrics #1 and #2, cut or tear one 18" x 22" piece of each fabric. Refer to the General Instructions section of this book (pages 11-22) and combine the fabric pieces to make one-inch finished triangle-squares. Use Grid #13 for your marking pattern, marking a grid of 1⅞" squares.

The Grid #13 arrangement makes 198 triangle-squares. The Mini Wall Quilt requires 160 triangle-squares, so you will have a few pieces left over.

III. Make Single Triangles. The Mini Wall Quilt requires 64 single triangles (32 of each fabric) for the Ocean Waves units. To make the single triangles, cut 16 1⅞" squares from each fabric. Cut each square in half diagonally to make two single triangles.

IV. Cut Setting Pieces. Cut the 2⅞" strips of Fabric #1 and Fabric #2 into eight 2⅞" squares. Cut the squares in half diagonally to make 16 D setting triangles of each fabric.

V. Follow instructions V through VII for the Wall Quilt to complete Mini Wall Quilt.

Quilting

Planning and Marking the Quilting

The setting pieces on Ocean Waves quilts are nice open areas to show off fancy quilting. On the following pages are some suggested quilting designs for the A setting squares. Refer to the photographs for ideas on how to adapt these designs for the setting triangles.

Trace a design onto paper with a permanent felt-tip pen. Center a setting square over the design. The design will show through all but the darkest fabrics. Then, lightly trace the design onto the fabric with chalk or a pencil. For dark fabrics, make templates or stencils to mark the quilting designs on the quilt top.

A suggested quilting pattern for the patchwork triangles is shown (Figure 1). The design provides adquate quilting for the patchwork pieces but is not as time consuming as outline quilting each individual triangle. Quilt the design either ¼-inch from the seams or "in the ditch" along the seam lines. It is not necessary to mark this quilting design since it follows the patchwork seams.

Piecing the Quilt Back

Plan the size of your quilt back to be at least three inches larger on all four sides than the quilt top. The quilt backs for the Doll quilts and Mini-Wall quilts can be cut from one fabric width and do not require piecing. For the larger quilts, cut or tear the backing fabric into two equal lengths. Split one length in half, lengthwise. Matching selvages and taking ½-inch seams, sew a half-panel to each side of a full panel. Press the seams to one side; trim the seam allowances to ¼ inch.

Basting the Quilt

Tape the quilt back to the floor or to a large table-top with the wrong side of the back facing up, or tack the quilt back to a large quilting frame. Carefully spread the batting on the back. Lay the quilt top atop the batting, centering it and smoothing out wrinkles. Baste along the rows of triangle-squares, adding additional basting as necessary.

Quilting the Quilt

Quilting stitches are small running stitches through all three layers of the quilt. The stitches should be small, straight, and uniform; stitches on the quilt back should look the same as stitches on the quilt top.

Begin quilting at the center of the quilt and work toward the edges. Pinning or basting a small terry-cloth towel to the quilt edge will help hold the quilt edges in a hoop and help prevent them from stretching while quilting.

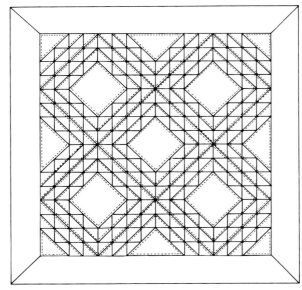

Figure 1

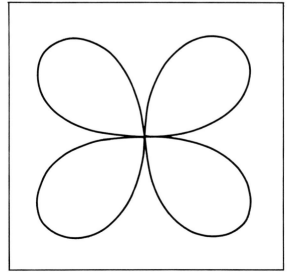